To _____

From _____

Date _____

Rescued from the archives of the 1830's by
DAVID HOFFMAN

A NEW
HIEROGLYPHICAL
BIBLE.

◆

WITH
FOUR HUNDRED
EMBELLISHMENTS
ON WOOD.

ELEVENTH EDITION.

CHISWICK :

PRINTED BY C. WHITTINGHAM,
FOR WILLIAM JACKSON.
NEW-YORK.

1836.

AMERICAN HERITAGE PRESS   NEW YORK

ADVERTISEMENT.

HIEROGLYPHICS originated with the ancient Egyptians. They were invented and adopted by the priests and sages of that country, to conceal as well as to conserve the knowledge of truth; but they are here employed to engage the mind, by attracting the eye, and by this means to impress on the recollection the most interesting passages of Holy Writ. Amusement is here designed to subserve the more important ends of instruction.

The professed aim of the present work, indeed, is to promote an early love for the Sacred Writings in the minds of youth, by alluring attention towards them, and thus assisting both parents and teachers in the arduous duty of training and disciplining the rising generation in ' the nurture and admonition of the Lord.'

Impressed with this view, it will be perceived that much regard has been paid, during the compilation of these pages, to the character of the selections made from the Word of God; such parts being preferred, for illustration and embellishment, as were either thought to contain the most momentous truths or the most interesting relations. The correct reading of each emblematical verse, pointed out by Italics, will be found at the bottom of every page. Reference to the words distinguished by the Italic type, therefore, will at once explain the nature of the hieroglyphic.

It appears quite unnecessary to dwell on the utility of the present Work, which must be obvious to every one.

Respecting the execution of it, however, the Proprietors would flatter themselves with having taken some pains to improve on the appearance of publications of the same stamp; and that, concerning the embellishments and typography, this Edition is decidedly superior to any that has hitherto been submitted to the public.

And God said, Let us make man in
our image, after our likeness; and
let them have dominion

over the  of the sea,

and over the of the air,

and over the  and

over all the earth, and over every creeping thing that creepeth upon the earth.

And God said, Let us make man in our image
after our likeness; and let them have dominion
over the *fish* of the sea, and over the *fowl* of the
air, and over the *cattle*, and over all the earth,
and over every creeping thing that creepeth upon
the earth.

And the rib, which the

 God had taken

from made he a

and brought her unto

the

And the rib, which the *Lord* God had taken from *man*, made he a *woman*, and brought her unto the *man*.

Now the  was

more subtle than any

 of the field

which the Lord had made: and he
said unto the

 Yea, hath God said, Ye
shall not
eat of
every
of the garden.

Now the *serpent* was more subtle than any
beast of the field which the Lord God had
made: and he said unto the *woman*, Yea, hath
God said, Ye shall not eat of every *tree* of the
garden.

And I will put enmity between

 and the

and between thy seed and her seed;

it shall bruise thy

 and thou shalt
bruise his

And I will put enmity between *thee* and the
woman, and between thy seed and her seed; it
shall bruise thy *head*, and thou shalt bruise his
heel.

But the found no rest

for the sole of her

and she returned unto him into the

 for the

waters

were on

the  of the whole earth.

Then he put forth his

and took her, and pulled her in unto
him into the ark.

But the *dove* found no rest for the sole of her
foot, and she returned unto him into the *ark:*
for the waters were upon the *face* of the whole
earth. Then he put forth his *hand*, and took her,
and pulled her in unto him into the ark.

And I have

and  flocks, and

 servants, and

servants: and I have sent to tell my
lord, that I may find grace in thy
sight.

And I have *oxen*, and *asses*, flocks, and *men*
servants, and *women* servants: and I have sent to
tell my lord, that I may find grace in thy sight.

And Pharaoh's was in my

hand: and I took

the  and pressed them

into Pharaoh's cup, and I gave the cup

into  's hand.

And Pharaoh's *cup* was in my hand: and I took the *grapes*, and pressed them into Pharaoh's cup, and I gave the cup into *Pharaoh's* hand.

And  and went

in unto Pharoah, and they did so as

the  had commanded :

and Aaron cast down his rod before

 and before his servants,

and it became a

And *Moses* and *Aaron* went in unto Pharaoh, and they did so as the *Lord* had commanded : and Aaron cast down his rod before *Pharoah*, and before his servants, and it became a *serpent*.

And the of God, which

went before the

of Israel, removed and went behind
them; and

the pillar of the

went from before their face, and stood
behind them.

And the *angel* of God, which went before the
camp of Israel, removed and went behind them;
and the pillar of the *cloud* went from before
their face, and stood behind them.

Thou shalt not covet thy neighbour's

 thou shalt not covet

thy neighbour's   nor his man-

servant, nor his maid-servant, nor his

 nor his

nor any thing that is thy neighbour's.

Thou shalt not covet thy neighbour's *house*, thou shalt not covet thy neighbour's *wife*, nor his man-servant, nor his maid-servant, nor his *ox*, nor his *ass*, nor any thing that is thy neighbour's.

And the shall take of

the blood of the sin offering wit h his finger, and put it upon the

 of the

of burnt offering, and shall pour out his blood at the bottom of the altar of burnt offering.

And the *priest* shall take of the blood of the sin offering with his finger, and put it upon the *horns* of the *altar* of burnt offering, and shall pour out his blood at the bottom of the altar of burnt offering.

Then the Lord opened the

 of Balaam, and he saw

the of the

standing in the way,

and his  drawn in

his hand: and he bowed down

his and fell flat on his face.

Then the Lord opened the *eyes* of Balaam,
and he saw the *angel* of the *Lord* standing in
the way, and his *sword* drawn in his hand: and
he bowed down his *head*, and fell flat on his face.

O that there were such

an in them, that they would

fear me, and keep all my

always, that it might be well with
them, and with

their  for ever.

O that there were such an *heart* in them, that
they would fear me, and keep all my *command-
ments* always, that it might be well with them,
and with their *children* for ever.

And as they that bare

the  were come

unto Jordan, and the feet of

the  that bare the ark

were dipped in the brim of the water,
for Jordan overfloweth all his banks
all the time of

And as they that bare the *ark* were come unto
Jordan, and the feet of the *priests* that bare the
ark were dipped in the brim of the water, for
Jordan overfloweth all his banks all the time of
harvest.

Speak to the  of

Israel, saying, Appoint out for you

of refuge, whereof I spake unto

you by the of

Speak to the *children* of Israel, saying, Appoint out for you *cities*, of refuge, whereof I spake unto you by the *hand* of *Moses*.

So Manoah took a with a

meat offering, and offered it upon

a  unto the Lord:

and the did wondrously;

and and his

looked on.

So Manoah took a *kid*, with a meat offering, and offered it upon a *rock* unto the Lord: and the *angel* did wondrously; and *Manoah* and his *wife* looked on.

And the men of the city said unto him on the seventh day, before the went down, What is sweeter than honey? and what is

stronger than a  And he

said unto them, If ye had not

 ye had not with my found out my riddle.

And the men of the city said unto him on the seventh day, before the *sun* went down, What is sweeter than honey? and what is stronger than a *lion?* And he said unto them, If ye had not *ploughed* with my *heifer*, ye had not found out my riddle.

And she said, I pray you, let me

and gather after the

among

the

so she came, and hath continued even
from the morning until now, that she
tarried a little in the

And she said, I pray you, let me *glean* and
gather after the *reapers* among the *sheaves:* so
she came, and hath continued even from the
morning until now, that she tarried a little in the
house.

And  said unto Saul, Thy

servant kept his father's

 and there came

a  and a

 and took
a

out of the flock.

And *David* said unto Saul, Thy servant kept his father's *sheep*, and there came a *lion*, and a *bear*, and took a *lamb* out of the flock.

And the young that told

him, said, As I happened by chance upon Mount Gilboa, behold, Saul leaned upon his spear: and, lo,

the  and

 followed

hard after him.

And the young *man* that told him said, As I happened by chance upon Mount Gilboa, behold, Saul leaned upon his spear: and, lo, the *chariots* and *horsemen* followed hard after him.

And they brought every

his present,

of silver, and vessels of gold, and

garments, and

and spices,

and mules, a rate year by year.

And they brought every *man* his present, *vessels* of silver, and vessels of gold, and garments, and *armour*, and spices, *horses*, and mules, a rate year by year.

Let us make a little chamber, I pray

thee, on the

and let us set for him there a

 and a

and a and a and it shall

be, when he cometh to us, that he

shall turn in thither.

Let us make a little chamber, I pray thee, on
the *wall*; and let us set for him there a *bed*, and
a *table*, and a *stool*, and a *candlestick*: and it
shall be, when he cometh to us, that he shall
turn in thither.

And he dealt to every one of Israel,

both and to every

one a  of bread, and a good

piece of and a

 of wine.

And he dealt to every one of Israel, both *man* and *woman*, to every one a *loaf* of bread, and a good piece of *flesh*, and a *flagon* of wine.

They smote also the

of

and carried away

 and

in abundance, and returned to
Jerusalem.

They smote also the *tents* of *cattle*, and carried away *sheep* and *camels* in abundance, and
returned to Jerusalem.

Blessed be the  God

of our which hath put such

a thing as this in the king's

to beautify the

of the Lord which is in Jerusalem.

Blessed be the *Lord* God of our *fathers*, which hath put such a thing as this in the king's *heart*, to beautify the *house* of the Lord which is in Jerusalem.

But the  gate did

the sons of Hassenaah build, who also laid the beams thereof, and set

up the  thereof,

the  thereof,

and the bàrs thereof.

But the *fish*-gate did the sons of Hassenaah build, who also laid the beams thereof, and set up the *doors* thereof, the *locks* thereof, and the bars thereof.

Let the royal apparel be brought

which the  useth to wear,

and the

that the king rideth upon, and the

 royal which is set upon his
head.

Let the royal apparel be brought which the *king* useth to wear, and the *horse* that the king rideth upon, and the *crown* royal which is set upon his head.

Shall mortal man be more

than God? shall a man

be more pure than his Maker?
Behold, he put no trust

in his   and his

he chargeth with folly

Shall mortal man be more *just* than God?
shall a man be more pure than his Maker?
Behold, he put no trust in his *servants,* and his
angels he chargeth with folly.

By his  he hath

garnished the heavens;

his hath

formed the crooked

By his *spirit* he hath garnished the heavens;
his *hand* hath formed the crooked *serpent*.

I went mourning without the

I stood up, and I cried in the
congregation.   I am a

brother to

and a companion to

,

I went mourning without the *sun:* I stood up
and I cried in the congregation.   I am a brother
to *dragons,* and a companion to *owls.*

I know all the

of the

and the  of the

 are mine.

I know all the *fowls* of the *mountains:* and
he *wild beasts* of the *field* are mine.

He sent divers sorts of

among them, which devoured them;

and  which

destroyed them.   He gave also their

increase unto the

and their labour unto the

He sent divers sorts of *flies* among them, which devoured them; and *frogs*, which destroyed them. He gave also their increase unto the *caterpillar*, and their labour unto the *locust*.

The high hills are
a refuge for the

and the

for the  He appointeth

the moon for seasons: the

knoweth his going down.

The high hills are a refuge for the *wild goats*,
and the *rocks* for the *conies*. He appointeth the
moon for seasons: the *sun* knoweth his going
down.

Thy wife shall be as a fruitful

by the sides of thine

   thy

like olive plants round about thy

Thy wife shall be as a fruitful *vine* by the sides of thine *house:* thy *children* like olive plants round about thy *table.*

Praise him with the sound of the

 praise him with the

psaltery and Praise him

with the timbrel and dance: praise him with stringed instruments and

 s.

Praise him with the sound of the *trumpet:* praise him with the psaltery and *harp.* Praise him with the timbrel and dance: praise him with stringed instruments and *organs.*

A wise scattereth the

wicked, and bringeth the

over them.   The spirit of man is the

 of the

searching all the inward parts of the
belly.

A wise *king* scattereth the wicked, and bringeth the *wheel* over them.   The spirit of man is
the *candle* of the *Lord,* searching all the inward
parts of the belly.

 for the

a bridle for the

A

and a for the

fool's back.

A *whip* for the *horse*, a bridle for the *ass*, and a *rod* for the fool's back.

He that observeth the

shall not

and he that regardeth

the

shall not

He that observeth the *wind* shall not *sow;* and he that regardeth the *clouds* shall not *reap*.

His is as the most fine

gold, his locks are bushy, and black

as a His

are as the eyes of by the

rivers of waters, washed with milk,
and fitly set.

His *head* is as the most fine gold, his locks
are bushy and black as a *raven*.   His *eyes* are as
the eyes of *doves* by the rivers of waters, washed
with milk, and fitly set.

Then flew one of the

unto me,

having a live coal in his

which he had taken with the

off the

Then flew one of the *seraphims* unto me, having a live coal in his *hand*, which he had taken with the *tongs* from off the *altar*.

The also shall dwell

with the lamb, and the

shall lie down with the kid: and the

 and the young

and the fatling together; and a little

 shall lead them.

The *wolf* also shall dwell with the lamb, and the *leopard* shall lie down with the kid: and the *calf*, and the young *lion*, and the fatling together; and a little *child* shall lead them.

Woe to them that go down to Egypt

for help; and stay on

and trust in

because they are many; and in

because they are

very strong: but they look not unto
the Holy One of Israel, neither seek
the Lord.

Woe to them that go down to Egypt for help;
and stay on *horses*, and trust in *chariots*, because
they are many; and in *horsemen*, because they
are very strong: but they look not unto the Holy
One of Israel, neither seek the Lord.

The sin of Judah is written with a of iron, and with

the point of a diamond: it is graven

upon the of their

 and upon the

of your altars.

The sin of Judah is written with a *pen* of iron, and with the point of a diamond: it is graven upon the *table* of their *heart*, and upon the *horns* of your altars.

He hath bent his like an

enemy: he stood with his right hand
as an adversary, and slew all that

were pleasant to the in the

tabernacle of the of Zion: he

poured out his fury like

He hath bent his *bow* like an enemy: he stood
with his right hand as an adversary, and slew
all that were pleasant to the *eye* in the tabernacle of the *daughter* of Zion: he poured out his
fury like *fire*.

As for the likeness of their faces, they

four had the of a man and

the face of a  on

the right side; and they four had the

face of an  on the left

side: they four also had the face of

an

As for the likeness of their faces, they four
had the *face* of a man, and the face of a *lion* on
the right side; and they four had the face of an
ox on the left side: they four also had the face
of an *eagle*.

Then said these  We

shall not find any occasion against this

 except we find it

against him concerning the law of his
God.

Then said these *men*, We shall not find any
occasion against this *Daniel*, except we find it
against him concerning the law of his *God*.

I will meet them as a

 that is bereaved of

her whelps, and will rend the caul of

their and there will I devour

them like a

the wild beast shall tear them.

I will meet them as a *bear* that is bereaved of
her whelps, and will rend the caul of their *heart*,
and there will I devour them like a *lion*: the
wild beast shall tear them.

The  shall quake

before them; the

shall tremble: the and the

 shall be dark,
and the

shall withdraw their shining.

The *earth* shall quake before them; the *heavens* shall tremble: the *sun* and the *moon* shall be dark, and the *stars* shall withdraw their shining.

Thus saith the LORD; As the shepherd taketh out of the mouth of

the lion two or a piece

of an so shall the children

of Israel be taken out that dwell in
Samaria in the corner of a bed, and
in Damascus in a

Thus saith the Lord; As the shepherd taketh
out of the mouth of the lion two *legs*, or a piece
of an *ear;* so shall the children of Israel be
taken out that dwell in Samaria in the corner of
a bed, and in Damascus in a *couch.*

Though thou exalt thyself as the

 and though thou set thy

 among the

thence will I bring thee down, saith the

Though thou exalt thyself as the *eagle*, and
though thou set thy *nest* among the *stars*, thence
will I bring thee down, saith the *Lord*.

But the  sent out a

great  into the

sea, and there was a mighty tempest

in the  so

that the  was like

to be broken.

But the *Lord* sent out a great *wind* into the sea, an there was a mighty tempest in the *sea*, so that the *ship* was like to be broken.

The  thereof judge for

reward, and the

thereof teach for hire, and the

 thereof divine for

money: yet will they lean upon the Lord, and say, Is not the Lord among us? none evil can come upon us.

The *heads* thereof judge for reward, and the *priests* thereof teach for hire, and the *prophets* thereof divine for money: yet will they lean upon the Lord, and say, Is not the Lord among us? none evil can come upon us.

The noise of a

and the noise of the rattling of the

 and of the prancing of

 and of the

jumping

The noise of a *whip*, and the noise of the rattling of the *wheels*, and of the prancing of *horses*, and of the jumping *chariots*.

Thou art of purer

than to behold evil, and canst not look on iniquity: wherefore lookest thou upon them that deal treacherously,

and holdest thy when the

wicked devoureth the

  that is more

than he?

Thou art of purer *eyes* than to behold evil, and canst not look on iniquity: wherefore lookest thou upon them that deal treacherously, and holdest thy *tongue* when the wicked devoureth the *man* that is more *righteous* than he?

And the sea

shall be dwellings and

for

and folds for

And the sea *coast* shall be dwellings and *cottages* for *shepherds,* and folds for *flocks.*

For thus saith the  of

Hosts, Yet once, it is a little while, and

I will shake the

and the  and the

 and the dry land.

For thus saith the *Lord* of Hosts, Yet once, it is a little while, and I will shake the *heavens,* and the *earth,* and the *sea,* and the dry land.

And so shall be the plague of the

of the
the

of the   and of

the  and of all the

beasts that shall be in these

 as this plague.

And so shall be the plague of the *horse*, of the *mule*, of the *camel*, and of the *ass*, and of all the beasts that shall be in these *tents*, as this plague.

But unto you that fear my name

shall the of

 arise with healing

in his and ye

shall go forth, and grow up as

 of the stall.

But unto you that fear my name shall the *Sun* of *righteousness* arise with healing in his *wings;* and ye shall go forth, and grow up as *calves* of the stall.

But while he thought on these things,

behold, the  of the

Lord appeared unto him in a dream,

     thou

saying   son of

fear not to take unto thee Mary thy

wife: for that which is conceived in

her is of the

But while he thought on these things, behold, the *angel* of the Lord appeared unto him in a dream, saying, *Joseph,* thou son of *David,* fear not to take unto thee Mary thy wife: for that which is conceived in her is of the *Holy Ghost.*

Whose is in his

 and he will throughly

purge his floor, and gather his

 into
the

but he will burn up the chaff with

unquenchable

Whose *fan* is in his *hand*, and he will throughly purge his floor, and gather his *wheat* into the *garner:* but he will burn up the chaff with unquenchable *fire*.

And  saith unto him, The

 have holes, and

the  of the

air have nests; but th eSon of

 hath not where to lay his
head.

And *Jesus* saith unto him, The *foxes* have holes,
and the *birds* of the air have nests; but the Son
of *man* hath not where to lay his head.

Behold, I send you forth as

in the midst of

be ye therefore wise as

and harmless as

Behold, I send you forth as *sheep* in the midst of *wolves:* be ye therefore wise as *serpents,* and harmless as *doves.*

And  spake to his

 that a small

 should wait on

him because of the multitude, lest
they should throng him.

And *Christ* spake to his *disciples*, that a small
ship should wait on him because of the multitude,
lest they should throng him.

And she answered and said unto

him, yes,

yet the

under the  eat of the

crumbs.

And she answered and said unto him, Yes,
Lord: yet the *dogs* under the *table* eat of the
children's crumbs.

And now also the is laid

unto the root of the trees: every

 therefore which

bringeth not forth good

 is  and

cast into the

And now also the *axe* is laid unto the root of
the trees: every *tree* therefore which bringeth
not forth good *fruit* is *hewn down*, and cast into
the *fire*.

And they shall scourge him, and put

him to  And the third

day he shall

again.

And they shall scourge him, and put him to
death: and the third day he shall *rise* again.

Saying, Blessed be the

 that cometh

in the name of the

in heaven, and glory in the
highest.

Saying, Blessed be the *King* that cometh in
the name of the *Lord: peace* in heaven, and
glory in the highest.

And found in the

those that sold

and

and

doves, and the

of money sitting.

And found in the *temple* those that sold *oxen*, and *sheep*, and doves, and the *changers* of money sitting.

 answered, Verily, verily,

I say unto thee, except a

be born of

and of the  he

cannot enter into the kingdom of God.

Jesus answered, Verily, verily, I say unto thee,
Except a *man* be born of *water* and of the *Spirit*,
he cannot enter into the kingdom of God.

But he that is an hireling, and not the

whose own the

are not, seeth the

coming, and

leaveth the sheep, and fleeth: and the wolf catcheth them, and scattereth the sheep.

But he that is an hireling, and not the *shepherd*, whose own the *sheep* are not, seeth the *wolf* coming, and leaveth the sheep, and fleeth: and the wolf catcheth them, and scattereth the sheep.

For it is written in the

of Psalms, Let his

be desolate, and let no man dwell

therein: and, his rick

let another take.

For it is written in the *book* of Psalms, Let his *habitation* be desolate, and let no man dwell therein: and, his *bishop*rick let another take.

For  speaketh

concerning him, I foresaw the

 always before

my for he is on my right

 that I should not be

moved.

For *David* speaketh concerning him, I foresaw
the *Lord* always before my *face;* for he is on my
right *hand,* that I should not be moved.

And daily in the

and in every  they

ceased not to teach and

 Jesus Christ.

And daily in the *temple*, and in every *house*, they ceased not to teach and *preach* Jesus Christ.

Upon the which when I had fastened

mine  I considered,

and saw four-footed

 of the earth, and

wild beasts, and

 and

 of the air.

Upon the which when I had fastened mine
eyes, I considered, and saw four-footed *beasts* of
the earth, and wild beasts, and *creeping things*,
and *fowls* of the air.

Then the

of

which was before their city, brought

and

unto the gates,

and would have done sacrifice with
the people.

Then the *priest* of *Jupiter* which was before
their city, brought *oxen* and *garlands* unto the
gates, and would have done sacrifice with the
people.

And as the shipmen were about to flee out of the ship, when they had let down the

into the

sea, under colour as though they

would have cast

out of the foreship.

And as the shipmen were about to flee out of the ship, when they had let down the *boat* into the sea, under colour as though they would have cast *anchor* out of the foreship.

For if by one

's offence

reigned by one; much more they
which receive abundance of

grace, and of the gift of

shall reign in life by one,

For if by one *man*'s offence, *Death* reigned
by one; much more they which receive abundance of grace, and of the gift of *righteousness*,
shall reign in life by one, *Jesus Christ.*

And  saith, Let

their be made a

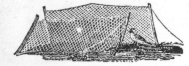 and a

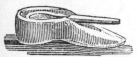 and a stumbling-

block, and a recompense unto them.

And *David* saith, Let their *table* be made a *snare*, and a *trap*, and a stumbling-block, and a recompense unto them.

Now the God of

fill you with all joy and

in believing,

that ye may abound in hope, through

the power of the

Now the God of *hope* fill you with all joy and
peace in believing, that ye may abound in hope,
through the power of the *Holy Ghost*.

For I think that God hath set forth

us the   last, as it

were appointed to   for we
are made

a spectacle unto the world, and to

and
to

For I think that God hath set forth us the
apostles last, as it were appointed to *death*: for
we are made a spectacle unto the world, and to
angels, and to *men*.

For it is written in the of

 Thou shalt not muzzle

the mouth of the

that treadeth out the

Doth God take care for oxen?

For it is written in the *law* of *Moses*, Thou shalt not muzzle the mouth of the *ox* that treadeth out the *corn*. Doth God take care for oxen?

For we know, that, if our earthly

of this

tabernacle were dissolved, we have a building of God, an house not made

with  eternal

in the

For we know, that, if our earthly *house* of this tabernacle were dissolved, we have a building of God, an house not made with *hands,* eternal in the *heavens.*

Be not deceived; God is not mocked:
for whatsoever a

that shall he also

Be not deceived; God is not mocked: for
whatsoever a *man soweth*, that shall he also *reap*.

That  may dwell in your

  by faith; that ye,

being rooted and grounded in

That *Christ* may dwell in your *hearts* by faith;
that ye, being rooted and grounded in *love.*

And I entreat thee also, true

fellow, help those

which laboured with

me in the gospel, with Clement also,
and with other my fellow-labourers,
whose names are in the

of

And I entreat thee also, true *yoke*-fellow, help those *women* which laboured with me in the gospel, with Clement also, and with other my fellow-labourers, whose names are in the *book* of *life*.

And having made through

the blood of his  by him to

reconcile all things unto himself; by

him, I say, whether they be things in

or things in

And having made *peace* through the blood of his *cross,* by him to reconcile all things unto himself; by him, I say, whether they be things in *earth,* or things in *heaven.*

For the

himself shall descend from heaven with a shout, with the voice of the

arch-  and with the

 of God : and the

dead in  shall rise first.

For the *Lord* himself shall descend from heaven with a shout, with the voice of the arch-*angel*, and with the *trump* of God : and the dead in *Christ* shall rise first.

We are bound to thank God always

for you,   as it is

meet, because that your

groweth exceedingly, and the

of every one of you

all toward each other aboundeth.

We are bound to thank God always for you, *brethren*, as it is meet, because that your *faith* groweth exceedingly, and the *charity* of every one of you all toward each other aboundeth.

For if a  know not how

to rule his own

how shall he take care of the

 of God?

For if a *man* know not how to rule his own *house*, how shall he take care of the *church* of God?

Only  is with me.

Take  and

bring him with thee: for he is
profitable to me for the

Only *Luke* is with me. Take *Mark*, and bring
him with thee: for he is profitable to me for the
ministry.

Not by works of  which

we have done, but according to his

mercy  saved us, by the

washing of regeneration, and renewing

of the

Not by works of *righteousness* which we have
done, but according to his mercy *he* saved us,
by the washing of regeneration, and renewing of
the *Holy Ghost*.

Yet, for  sake, I

rather beseech thee, being such an one

 as   the aged, and now also a

 of

Yet, for *love's* sake, I rather beseech thee, being such an one as *Paul* the aged, and now also a *prisoner* of *Jesus Christ*.

Yet Michael the arch-

when contending

with the

he disputed

about the
body of

durst not
bring against

him a railing
accusation,
but said, The

rebuke
thee.

Yet Michael the arch-*angel*, when contending with the *devil*, he disputed about the body of *Moses*, durst not bring against him a railing accusation, but said, The *Lord* rebuke thee.

And the beast which I saw was like

unto a  and his

feet were as the feet of a

 and his mouth as

the mouth of a

and the  gave

him his power, and his seat, and
great authority.

And the beast which I saw was like unto a
leopard, and his feet were as the feet of a *bear*,
and his mouth as the mouth of a *lion:* and the
dragon gave him his power, and his seat, and
great authority.

THE PENNY MAGAZINE, for 1835.

Of the early volumes of this work, so well known, and so justly appreciated, upwards of 63,000 copies have been printed and sold in the United States, and in England, its regular circulation has exceeded 200,000. It still continues to be published under the auspices of "*The Society for the Diffusion of Useful Knowledge,*" a Society instituted by men of the most eminent rank and talent, for the purpose of distributing information and instruction in the cheapest form. The subjects which have uniformly been treated, have been striking points of Natural History; Accounts of the great Works of Art in Sculpture and Painting; Descriptions of Antiquities; Personal Narratives of Travellers; Biographies of Eminent Men; Elementary principles of Languages and Numbers; Established Facts in Statistics and Political Economy.

Subscribers' names are received by all booksellers, and by the Publisher,
WILLIAM JACKSON, 53 *Cedar-street.*

Under the Direction of the Society for the Diffusion of Useful Knowledge.

THE PENNY CYCLOPÆDIA,

VOL. IV.

Bound in embossed cloth or leather to match the three first Volumes; price $2,00.

From the Advertisement to the Sixth Volume.

A publication such as this, aiming at the union of excellence with cheapness, requires the support of a very large body of purchasers. The continuance of this support must, however, in great part, depend upon the Cyclopædia being completed within a reasonable period, and in a moderate number of volumes; it being borne in mind at the same time, that no rate of publication must be attempted which may prevent the careful revision of every portion of the work, and that no scale as to the length of the articles must be adopted which would destroy their usefulness. It has been the constant endeavour of the Editor, and the gentlemen who contribute to the Cyclopædia, to render the articles as concise as was compatible with preserving their value; and experience will now enable them to effect this object more completely than it has already been done. Added to this, many of the articles already published are necessary of greater length than the majority of those which are to come; for advantage has been taken, in most cases to explain the general principles of a subject on the first notice of a word connected with it; and in many instances it has been considered advisable to give under one head or title such a general view of a subject as will render it sufficient in many subsequent heads or titles to refer to the general article. Without any material alteration of the present scale as regards the length of the more important articles, the Committee feel assured that *somewhat more than a fourth of the whole Cyclopædia is now published;* and they therefore propose that the work shall be completed in Eighteen Volumes of the present size, and they pledge themselves that it shall not exceed Twenty Volumes. Having settled these limits, the Committee look forward with confidence to the production of a work, which will be useful to the most critical student by its completeness and accuracy, and will present a vast body of information, at the cheapest rate, to those who are seeking for knowledge in a popular form.

In order to comply with the wishes of the bulk of the Subscribers to the Cyclopædia, it is the intention of the Committee, upon the completion of the letter B, to publish at the rate of *three volumes annually*, instead of two ; so that the *entire work may be published in little more than four years from the present time.* In making this announcement as to an increased speed in publication, and giving this pledge as to limitation of quantity, the Committee and the Publishers beg it to be understood, that they consider these arrangements as final.

WILLIAM JACKSON, 53 *Cedar Street.*

This day is Published, Price 50 Cents, neatly bound in cloth.

THE

PAINTER'S, GILDER'S,

AND

VARNISHER'S MANUAL:

Containing Rules and Regulations in every thing relating to the Arts of Painting, Gilding, and Varnishing ; numerous useful and valuable Receipts ; Tests for detecting Adulterations in Oils, Colours, &c., and a Statement of the Diseases and Accidents to which Painters, Gilders, and Varnishers, are peculiarly liable ; with the simplest and best Methods of Prevention and Remedy.

WILLIAM JACKSON, 53 *Cedar Street.*

Just Published, Price 75 Cents, neatly bound in cloth.

THE

BUILDER'S POCKET MANUAL ;

Containing the Elements of Building, Surveying, and Architecture ; with Practical Rules and Instructions in Carpentry, Bricklaying, Masonry, &c. ; Observations on the Properties of Materials, and a variety of Useful Tables and Receipts. With Twelve Plates. By A. C. SMEATON, Civil Engineer.

WILLIAM JACKSON, *Cedar Street.*

Just Published, embellished with numerous Engravings, and handsomely bound in embossed cloth, or half-bound calf, price $2,00.

THE SATURDAY MAGAZINE,

FOR 1835.

Published under the direction of the Society for the Promotion of Christian Knowledge.

WILLIAM JACKSON, *Cedar Street.*